MW01274683

POCKET MANNERS

Dining & Etiquette Guidelines at Your Fingertips!

SYLVIA McLAREN-TISHLER

Frameworks Publishing
Richmond, British Columbia

First Edition
First Printing, 2008

Book design, edit and layout by Charlene Murphy of GoodLife Publishing.

Framework Publishing
Richmond, British Columbia
frameworks-training.com

Books are available at quantity discounts. For more information please submit an email to info@frameworks-training.com.

POCKET MANNERS

*Dining & Etiquette Guidelines
at Your Fingertips!*

*This book is dedicated to my greatest accomplishments—
Jennifer, Mady and Eric, who learned their lessons
well. And to Mercedes, Grace, Finn, Jackson and Reed
for when Grammy can't be with you.*

To my elegant husband, who always impresses me.

CONTENTS

INTRODUCTION

Picture the following scenario in your mind: Your future in-laws/boss has invited you to their "summer" home in the Hamptons for the weekend along with several other friends and relatives. The weekend itinerary goes something like this:

Friday Night: Cocktail party
Saturday: Golf, tennis or boating
Saturday Evening: Cocktails at 7; Dinner at 8
(formal attire)
Sunday: Brunch around the pool

OK, so this is not your average invitation. Maybe it is just your boss inviting you to dinner, or you are going to a wedding or meeting your girlfriend/ boyfriends' parents for the first time. What it is—is a stressful, panic inducing situation and definitely a time to polish your manners and learn the proper protocol.

Most of us do not have the time to research proper etiquette for several different situations, but if you have your small *Pocket Manners* book you could quickly flip through its pages and get all the basics you need to relieve those jitters.

Pop the book into your handbag or inside pocket. When you're met with a challenge, dash into the rest room and quickly find a solution.

Not since your mother has anyone told you to mind your manners. You may lose a job opportunity, a sale or a perspective mate because of your manners, the way you dress or how you speak. The sad truth is no one will tell you. It is up to you to know and to practice good manners so you don't miss some of life's great opportunities.

I can help. I will take you through various scenarios from making a good first impression, working the room at a cocktail reception, navigating the cutlery at a formal dinner and many other helpful protocol guidelines like tipping, thank-you cards and netiquette.

INVITATIONS

RSVP: "Respondez, s'il vous Plait"
or "Please reply."

A response to an invitation should be given whether you can attend or not, and given within three days— a week at the very latest of receiving the invitation. This lets the hostess or event planner know how many people to count on and how much food and drink to supply.

"Regrets Only" means only those who are declining the invitation need to respond. Make sure you do.

FIRST IMPRESSIONS COUNT

What you wear to the company dinner or to your future in-laws for the weekend can make you or break you.

Dress to what the invitation calls for; formal attire, casual, casually elegant. Always dress one step above what you would normally wear. Leave your flip-flops and Birkenstocks at home unless you are going to a picnic on the beach.

Make sure your shirt is pressed, if you don't own an iron or know how to use one, have them professionally pressed. Raggedy collars and cuffs, stained ties, too short skirts, warn down shoes and chipped nail polish will give the impression of someone who doesn't care about their appearance and shows disrespect to a formal occasion and to the hostess.

Stand tall, walk confidently, eyes forward, shake hands confidently, yet warmly. Smile; look happy to be there.

Cleavage seems to be the acceptable look of the day. I know the men are loving it. But for work or professional occasions, the only cleavage that should be shown is the one between your toes. Evening occasions still call for restraint. Make sure you can't see all the way down to Victoria!

Do not chew gum, carry breath mints instead.

If you are out to impress, everything about you should look shiny and new...polished.

Think before you speak. Watch your language, and I don't just refer to off color words. Be careful with opinions and words like, "fat," "bald" and "unemployed." And don't ask, "When is your baby due?"

I once met with a man I hadn't seen for years. His opening remark to me was, "Well, you look fat and healthy!" Imagine the look on my face!

What is your body language saying about you? Are you open and receptive or closed off and defensive? Confident or cowardly?

Do not invade a person's personal space. Stand at arms length apart.

Wear very little, if any, cologne or perfume. Many people are allergic to scent these days and some scents are very strong and offensive. Ask a friend if your scent is too strong if you are unsure.

Use deodorant—sounds obvious, but think of those you've met who didn't. Reapply at the end of the day if necessary. Remember perspiration odors are attached to your clothes, so change your shirt and dry clean suits often if your perspire heavily. If you tend to perspire heavily, men should wear an undershirt to help in the blotting and women can use underarm pads.

Manicures don't have to be expensive, but keep your nails clean and neatly trimmed, not bitten to the quick. Ladies, if you choose polish, make sure it is fresh and unchipped, on both fingers and toes.

Men, remove your hat indoors.

Keep your tattoos covered in business.

Do I have to say, "Don't smoke"? But if you must, refresh your breath before you enter the room. Unfortunately it is difficult to erase, as smoke tends to infuse your clothes, your car, you hair, your skin as well as your breath. So if you really want to impress, try to give it up. I know it's difficult, but so worth it for many, many reasons.

Sign up for a public speaking class to help you become a more confident and eloquent speaker. May I recommend my *Public Speaking for the Terrified Pocket Tips*?

HOUSE GUEST ETIQUETTE

Imagine yourself getting ready for weekend visitors. You have cleaned the house from top to bottom, scrubbed the bathrooms, washed linens, made up beds and made your home ready for the queen!

Your guests arrive early, empty handed, starving and with their dog they forgot to mention. You continued to work the entire weekend cooking, serving and cleaning up. Sunday arrives and they finally leave, so you can clean everything all over again and restock the fridge.

Everyone has had a great time but you. As your guests drive away, your husband says, "Come and stay with us anytime. Come back soon!"

Sagging, exhausted at the front door you suddenly remember that old Ben Franklin quote "House guests are like fish. They start to stink after three days!" "How right he is," you are thinking.

If only your guests had followed some of these guidelines of being a good house guest:

Don't take the phrases, "Mi casa es su casa" or "Make yourself at home" literally.

Let your host know when you will arrive. Do not arrive early unless you have an early flight connection and then let them know. On the other hand, don't just show up a day late.

Never arrive empty handed. A simple bottle of wine is fine, a bouquet of flowers or a plant is even better. If you drink a particular beverage, bring it as well.

Take your shoes off at the door. Bring a pair of house slippers for comfort.

If you are on a specific diet, let your hostess know and bring some items as well. Allergic to shell fish or peanuts? Let it be known in advance.

If you do have your pet with you, make sure you bring Rover's food, toys, and cleanup baggies. Bring the pet's kennel to sleep in at night, and do not let it run wild throughout the house or yard.

These guidelines go double for your children. Bring extra snacks and favorite toys and brush them up on their manners before you leave.

Bring all of your own toiletries—toothpaste, hair spray, shampoo, etc.

Don't snoop in bathroom vanities, cupboards or anywhere else in the house. Would you like people snooping through your things?

Keep in mind that this is not a hotel with people to clean up after you.

Clean up after yourself in the bathroom. Men, if you splash… clean the rim or floor with toilet paper and put the seat down when you're finished. Wipe around the sink with paper and flush away. Re-fold the towels.

If you are sharing a bathroom with the rest of the family, find out the morning schedules and fit yours in at the most convenient time.

Bring a robe. You never know who you will run into in the hallway in the middle of the night!

Help with meal preparation, and don't even ask if you can help with the clean up. Just get up and chip in.

Offer to take the dog out for a walk. The dog will love it and it will give both you and the host a little space.

Make your bed every morning and pick up after yourself. Keep all of your things neatly in your room.

If you're sleeping on the couch or hide a bed, make up your bed first thing in the morning and put your bedding and luggage in a neat pile in a corner out of the way of the rest of the family.

If you are staying longer than three or four days, ask if you can use the laundry facilities and wash your own bedding and towels. Ask for cleaning products to clean the bathroom.

At the end of your stay, strip the bed and put the dirty sheets at the end of the bed or directly in the laundry.

Don't keep your hosts up all night just because you are a night owl and don't sleep in late causing your hostess to make another breakfast and yet another clean up.

Take the host out for dinner one evening or purchase and prepare dinner. Ordering and paying for take-out works great too.

Be open to new experiences with foods and or traditions. Don't be afraid to try new things.

If your host family says grace before meals just silently bow your head.

Do not feel uncomfortable if you feel you would like to take a nap. Not only does it give your host a break, but also rejuvenates you. Same thing goes for going out to explore the town.

Your host may have to work during your visit, so make plans ahead of time on what you'd like to do. Rent a car or find out bus or subway schedules to go out on your own. Be as independent as you would be at home. Let them know your time schedule so they are not waiting on you for meals.

Don't put your feet on the furniture and use a coaster for your drinks. Don't hog the remote.

Accidents happen, but replace anything that you might damage.

Don't forget to send your thank you note after.

Giving a small gift when you leave is a particularly wonderful gesture. A lovely set of towels or something you have noticed your host could use or enjoy, tickets to the movies for the children and certificate at a local restaurant for the adults are some suggestions.

Your hosts have saved you a considerable amount of money that you would have spent at a hotel and have gone through a great deal of care and effort to make your stay comfortable, so let them know how much you appreciate them.

One last note: These rules apply to staying with family as well as friends. Follow these guidelines and you will be invited back every time.

HOSTESS GIFTS

Don't leave home without one. God forbid you should have to knock with your elbows!

Flowers and wine are always a welcome gift, but more original gift ideas like candles, home made candies or appetizers or a beautiful scarf for the hostess will surely impress.

If you are invited to a restaurant, rather than the couples' home for a celebration dinner, it is still good manners to bring a gift for the hostess.

If you don't want to be invited back, arrive late, empty handed, drink and eat everything in sight, and overstay your welcome.

COCKTAIL PARTY DOs & DON'Ts

Networking events are important if you want to be seen and remembered, and can definitely add to the success of your business. Even if you'd rather stay home and eat TV dinners on the couch, you need to be visible. So, push yourself, get out there and enjoy yourself!

Here are a few things that you should know before you leave:

• Eat first before leaving home, so you are not starving and head straight for the food table when you arrive. This allows you to mingle first and eat later. You won't have to juggle a food plate and wine glass, while trying to shake hands or carry on a conversation.

• Do not overindulge in the food, especially the

wine. We all know that loose lips sink ships. Always remember you are representing yourself and your company.

• Hors d'oeuvres are okay to eat with your fingers, but stay away from messy, drippy, or slurpy foods.

• Do not overload your plate; you can always go back for more.

✦ Hold your wine glass in your left hand, so you can shake with your right.

✦ Wear you name tag on your right, upper shoulder. People read from left to right. When you shake hands, you can look at a persons' name as you are shaking hands.

✦ Repeat their name at least three times during the conversation to help you to remember their name.

✦ Don't be a wallflower. Holding up the wall may make you feel secure, but you will look unapproachable. If you need to feel grounded, stand behind a couch or chair with just your finger-tips touching.

✦ When arriving to a party alone and you don't know anyone, walk up to the person closest to the door and introduce yourself.

✦ Do not overstay your welcome; keep mingling from one group to another.

✦ If you find two people deep in conversation, do

not interrupt. Pass them by for a group of three or four and join in.

+ Plan ahead your 30 second introduction that will tell people what you do.

+ Don't give away too much information. Allow room for the listener to ask you more questions like, "How do you do that?" or "How can you do that for me?"

• Try not to label yourself with "I'm a lawyer, or a teacher, or a realtor." Most times people will stop listening because they feel they know what you do. People want to know what you can do for them or what problems you can solve for them.

For instance, *"Hello, I'm Sylvia Tishler. I am the founder and director of Frameworks Finishing Academy. We offer courses in business protocol, dining decorum and etiquette, and public speaking. You already have great product. Let us polish your professionals to present your company in the best light possible."*

This can be broken up into a more conversational style but it leaves it open for questions and problem solving solutions.

• Polish up your listening and questions skills. Show genuine interest in others by asking open-ended questions to keep the conversation going.

• Welcome others into the group who look uncomfortable. Introduce yourself and then others will follow suit.

• If you are with someone you would rather not be and are having a difficult time extricating yourself, bringing another person into the group will give you the opportunity to slip away. Worse case scenario is to say you need to go to the rest room.

• I like to think of myself as the hostess of the evening—moving from group to group, introducing myself, meeting others and putting people together. The idea is to give something rather than waiting for others to come to you to entertain you.

• Make sure you have a good supply of business cards with you and pass them out freely. Ask for ones in return and the next day send a nice note by email and start up a mutual marketing campaign with them if it is suitable.

THE FORMAL DINNER

Being seated at the table set formally like this one can be a bit intimidating. Try to relax by remembering that the utensils are placed in the order of which they are used. That is, always begin with the fork farthest to the left at your place setting and move inward toward the plate with each subsequent course.

STEM WEAR

The water goblet is above and near the tip of the knife. The rest are arranged in relation to the water in an arch or v-shape. You may have a total of five glasses—champagne, wed wine, white wine, and sherry.

Sherry is drunk with the first course, the soup

course. White wine is traditionally for the fish course or poultry, red for meat and champagne for dessert. Again they are arranged in the order in which they will be used from right to left.

Each glass is removed after the course in which it is used, while the water glass stays in place for the entire meal and refilled as necessary.

If there is a place card above each place setting do not be tempted to change the seating arrangements.

The guest of honor always sits to the right of the hostess or host.

SAIL AWAY WITH SOUP

As the ship sails out to sea,
I spoon my soup away from me.

• Napkins: Wait until your host has been seated and has lifted his napkin, and then take yours and place it on your lap.

• If the napkin is large, fold it in half with the opening towards your knees; wipe your fingers on the inner fold to prevent soiling your clothing.

• Do not tuck your napkin in your collar.

• If you need to excuse yourself from the table, place your napkin on the seat or the arm of your chair.

• When you are finished with your meal, place the napkin to the left of your place setting, but not as originally folded.

- Do not place your napkin on top of the leftover food on your plate as a sign that you are finished.
- Do not blow your nose in your napkin, wipe your face, or wipe off your lipstick with it.
- Food is always passed to the right or counter-clockwise.
- Always pass the salt and pepper together, even if only one is asked for.
- Ladies, do not put your purse on the table. If it is small, put it behind your back. Do not hang it on the chair, to the left of the chair or on the floor, as the wait staff can trip on it. Put it under your chair.
- Do not apply your lipstick at the table or fix your hair. Slip to the ladies room for touch-ups.
- Never pick your teeth with your fork, knife, toothpick, sugar packet, or anything else. Excuse yourself and slip to the rest room. I have seen on too many occasions people actually using dental floss at the table! Ugh! Some people think that by covering their mouth with one hand while picking their teeth with a toothpick is acceptable—it is not!
- Do not overload your plate at the buffet or at the table. Take moderate portions and go back for seconds if necessary.

- Cleaning your plate is not necessary, but eating what you have served yourself is.
- Cutting your salad is perfectly fine.
- Bread should not be eaten wholly but broken into bite size pieces, butter it and then eat it.
- When taking the butter, take a small amount with the butter spreader on the butter plate and put it on your bread plate. Use your own butter knife.
- Do not dunk your bread into the soup or wipe your gravy with it.
- If you drop your fork on the floor, leave it there and ask the server for another.
- If you bite into a peace of gristle remove it with your fingers or your fork and put it on the side of your plate, not into your napkin, as you will then wipe it on your clothes or drop it on the floor.
- No double dipping.
- Wait until everyone is served before you begin; again wait for the host to begin.
- If you are with a large group, you may start when four or five people have been served.
- Do not hug your plate with both arms on the table shoveling the food in.
- Sit up straight both wrists gently resting on the table; bring your food to your mouth not the other way around.

- Slow down or speed up. If you are the last one to finish and everyone is waiting on you or if you are finished before anyone else is even half finished, this is for you.

- Keep the same speed as the rest of the people at the table. My husband and I once had dinner with another couple where the husband ate so fast he finished his entire meal before we barely got started and then went on to eat off his wife's plate. It was gross to watch.

- Spaghetti is one of my favourite meals, especially with meat balls. It has sent many outfits to the dry cleaners. Many Italian restaurants offer to put a napkin around your neck, which is perfectly fine. The proper way of eating long pasta is to twirl the pasta on a fork, using a large spoon as a guide for the fork. Don't cut your pasta with a knife and a fork.

IS THAT YOUR BUN OR MINE?

What if you spill your drink? Don't make a scene. Just summon the waiter for more napkins to clean up.

My friend, Neil, told me a story of going to a formal state dinner in Trinidad with his father when he was a teenager.

He was seated next to the mother of one of his friends, who was a beautiful Indian woman wearing a stunning white, silk sauri. Cornish game hens were on the menu, and when the man next to her cut into cut into his, it flew off his plate and landed in her lap!

She quickly picked up the hen, put it back on the man's plate, while he kept blustering on to his mates. She turned to Neil and said, "Please walk in front of me and take me to my car." Her gown was terribly soiled, but she did not make a scene.

She serenely and elegantly left the hall with Neil concealing the mess. She went home, changed and returned without the oaf next to her even noticing she was missing.

Neil was forever impressed at her stately manners.

NAVIGATING THE CUTLERY

Nothing shows poor upbringing faster than using the cutlery the wrong way. Follow these simple rules for optimal dining success!

• "Fork" has four letters and "left" has four letters, so it's easy to remember that forks are located on the left side of your plate.

• "Spoon" and 'knife" have five letters and "right" has five letters, so remember that knives and spoons are place on the right.

• The blade of the knife is always towards the plate.

• Always start from the outside and work your way in.

• Small forks and spoons placed above the plate are for dessert. They are brought down after your plate has been cleared and the dessert is about to be served.

• Your bread plate with its own bread knife is on the upper left side.

• Your stem wear are always on the right.

• If you pause during the meal, set your fork on the left side of your plate, with the tines down and the knife on the right with the sharp edge facing in.

• When you are resting between bites cross your fork and knife with the knife and fork pointing at 10 and 2.

• When you are finished eating, place your knife and fork beside each other on the right side diagonally across the plate tines facing up or down.

• A good wait staff will recognize the signals.

• A crucial rule: Once you pick up a utensil, it should never touch the table again. When you put it down place it on the plate, not on the table.

• Do not use your fork to cut everything on your plate. Soft foods are fine, but generally your knife and fork should work in tandem.

• Do not cut all your food into tiny pieces as you would for a child, but cut each piece as you are about to eat it.

• Must I say it? Don't talk with your mouth full!

AMERICAN VERSUS CONTINENTAL

North Americans practice what Emily Post called "zigzag eating." We cut our food with the fork in the left hand and the knife in the right, and then place the knife down on the plate and switch the fork to our right hand to eat. Through the course of a meal, the fork goes back and forth, from one hand to the other.

Europeans eat in what is called "Continental Style." They keep their forks in their left hands and eat with them that way, tines facing down.

Either method is acceptable.

HOSTING & TOASTING

- If you are the host or if you have been asked to choose the wine, ask the server for suggestions on what he would recommend.
- If you are concerned on how much to spend, discreetly point to a price on the wine list and tell the server you are looking for something like this. Anything between $30 and $60 is a safe bet.
- Serving white with fish and red with meat no longer applies. It's based more on the texture of the food.
- Check the bottle when it comes to the table, verify it is the wine you chose. If the label is stained, it is possible the wine is spoiled. Send it back.
- It is not necessary to smell the cork.
- Check the wine bouquet—swirl it, smell the

wine, and if it smells musty, or like damp cardboard, it is bad, so send it back. Once you taste it, it is your last chance to send it back.

• Always hold the wine glass by the stem or goblets under the bow. Holding the bowl with heat up the wine.

• If you don't drink just say, "No thank you." Ask for a soft drink if necessary or just water. Do not hold your hand over your glass.

DID YOU KNOW?

• Smoking prior to drinking wine affects the taste, as does chewing gum, eating breath mints or just brushed teeth. You can help by eating crackers first to cleanse the pallet.

• The host toasts the guest, during which the guest does not drink. The guest can then reciprocate with a toast and begin to drink. (Keep the toast short and sweet.)

• In medieval times clinking wine glasses was done to keep away evil spirits?

• When you hold your glass with your right hand, it is said the major artery to you heart runs down your right arm. So your toast is coming straight from the heart!

• A toast can be given at the beginning of the meal and then again during dessert.

WHAT & WHEN TO TIP

Nothing is more embarrassing to me than being out with someone who doesn't tip at all or is a cheap tipper. Worse yet is someone who complains loudly about the poor service to either get out of tipping or to get a free meal.

If you recognize yourself here and you are trying to make a good impression on your date, your boss or in laws, I suggest you follow these tips on tipping.

• First, check to see if the tip is already included in the total. Sometimes this will occur at large group functions.

• Do not tip on the tax.

• Food and drink - 15 to 20%

• Bartender - $1 a drink

- Food delivery - 10%
- Hotel bellman - $2 to $5
- Hotel room service - 15%
- Coat check - $1 to $2 per item
- Ladies room attendant - $1
- Hairdresser - 15% to 20%
- Manicurist and pedicurist - 10% to 20%
- Masseuse - 10% to 20%
- If the meal or the service was unsatisfactory, do not leave a tip, but quietly inform the manager or waiter. If neither is available, leave a note on the bill as to why. Making a scene only makes a fool of you and disrupts other peoples' meals.

THANK YOU NOTES

It's the small things that make a big impact. Don't forget to send a thank you note!

• Mail your note within 24 hours of the event.

• Make them short—three to five sentences.

• Don't use $20 words when a ten center is just as handy.

• Written thank you notes are not always necessary— it depends on the formality of the event. A phone call the next day or even an email works very well with friends and family.

• In the event of the weekend at the Hampton's where there is considerable preparation for your stay, requires a hand written note and mention of the attention to details by the hostess that made your visit so enjoyable.

- You may have a luncheon meeting where you have been given valuable advice. A thank you note showing your appreciation for the advice is most gracious.
- Use nice stationary and use your best penmanship.
- Sometimes just a bottle of wine with a thank you tag says it all.
- If you are a week late sending the thank you card, send it anyway; make light of the tardiness and concentrate on the gift or affair.

NETIQUETTE

A 21st century necessity! Yes we all love and need our cell phones and Blackberries, and they can provide ease and freedom in our day-to-day activities. But there is a time and a place. The following are guidelines and suggestions for courteous usage:

• Turn your cell phone off in a meeting, seminar, classroom, restaurant, bar, movie theatre, concert.

• Do not discuss your personal or professional problems, financial or health worries in public.

• Do not swear or have an argument on your cell in public.

• Lower your voice. No one is interested in what you have to say, and you are impressing no one.

• Turn off the speakerphone if others can hear you.

- It is not okay to speak at length on the bus, at the airport, or anywhere else where other passengers can't get away from you.
- Do not text message at the table, while having coffee with a friend or in a meeting! After all, it is just plain rude.
- Do not text message while driving. This is only common sense, but just the other day my friend was rear ended at a busy intersection in Los Angeles by a woman who was text messaging!

FUNNY STORY

I was at a Dionne Warwick concert this past year and while she was in the middle of one of her beautiful ballads, someone's cell phone went off.

She immediately stopped, looked out into the crowd to the flashing, offending cell phone, pointed her finger at the offending user and said, "Turn that thing off! After all, I came all this way just to see you!"

How perfect!

VOICE MAIL

Personal voice messages should include your name and company, if necessary, and the option for the person to leave a message. If you will be away from your voice mail box for an extended period of time, leave a message where you can be reached or when you will be returning. Long, cutsie songs or rapper messages precluding your message are annoying and leave an unprofessional message.

When leaving a voice message, be brief and speak slowly leaving your name, time of your call and a number where you can be reached. Repeating your number again at the end is very helpful.

EMAILS
• Emails should be brief without appearing rude.
• Always use the subject box to specify your message so you aren't deleted as spam.
• Emails are still business letters and therefore should be more formal if you want to make a good impression.
• Follow the letter protocol with a formal salutation, "Dear Mr. Jones."
• Always use your spell check and check for grammar.
• Create a signature line that has your name, business title and phone numbers.
• Do not SHOUT. Using all uppercase is considered Cyber Shouting. I know someone who uses all capitals because she says she can't see. I say

get stronger glasses or increase the font size on your computer.

• Also avoid sending messages in all lower case letters—they make you look like you have low self esteem.

• Some of my friends use "emoticons"—you know those bouncing happy faces and flashing hearts. One of my more creative friends actually writes full letters using the symbols for words. It's very cute and very clever, but gets very tiring. And just try reading it on a Blackberry where the pictures come through only as inscriptions. It's a nightmare!

• Use your BCC or Blind Carbon Copy, when sending an email to many email addresses. Otherwise you are sharing all the other email address, which is a breach in confidentiality and privacy.

• Be careful with the "Reply All" option as well. Reply only to the person who requires a response.

• Never say anything in an email you wouldn't say in public. Do not use off-colored words or gossip. Emails can be forwarded, duplicated and printed, so be careful where you want it to be seen.

CONCLUSION

So here we are back at the invitation to the weekend at the Hamptons. You sent your RSVP within three days of receiving your invitation, and here you are at the front door.

You look fantastic, pressed and polished, dressed casually elegant for the evening's cocktail party. You're right on time—not half hour early or a half hour late. In your weekender bag you have your *Pocket Manners* book, which your have read over and over, but brought it with you just in case. You have a bottle of scotch in one hand (the boss's favorite brand), a bouquet of white freesias in the other (boss's wife's favorite flower) and homemade dog biscuits for the family dog.

You schmoozed throughout the cocktail party,

mingling amongst the other guests and helped a few wallflowers feel more comfortable by taking them under your wing and introducing them to others. You did not over drink or over eat.

Saturday you chose to go golfing because that is where your boss was, and even though you are a really good golfer you let him win.

You showered and changed into an elegant, formal outfit for the dinner and were seated next to a tall, dark, handsome gentleman. (Bonus)

Your table manners were impeccable and you even helped the table mate next to you when he asked, "Is that your bun or mine?"

During dessert, you graciously proposed a toast to your boss's wife saying what a beautiful and elegant hostess she is.

You excused yourself early and arrived bright-eyed for brunch the next morning—looking again casually elegant, and you sat beside the handsome man again.

You made your formal farewells, thanking the host and hostess and asked the dark-eyed dream man for his phone number. You then drive away in your shiny, just detailed vehicle.

The very next day you send a hand-written thank you note attached to a dozen yellow roses to the hostess, telling her what a fabulous time you had.

Do I need to mention that you phoned the gorgeous man, who just happened to be the boss's favorite nephew?

Okay, so it's a little over the top, straight out of the *Young & The Restless*! But it could happen...

Mainly, it is a scenario where you will need to use all of your manners. This little *Pocket Manners* book will help you get through any situation.

You may choose to delve more deeply into business protocol and etiquette, and maybe learn about international etiquette, should you travel the world. If so, there are many good books on the market. One I highly recommend is *Business Class, Etiquette Essentials for Success at Work* by Jacqueline Whitmore.

Good manners will take you anywhere, get you invited to the best parties and mostly allow you to feel comfortable in any situation.

Don't let your manners hold you back from all the wonderful opportunities available to you. Don't leave it to chance because no one will ever tell you. You must learn it yourself.

Written by my friend Margaret, who has been a photo-journalist in East Africa for many years, is a story from her book, *Where the Tarmac Ends.*

Back in 1948, while my father-in-law and I lunched at the Royal Thames Yacht Club, in London (UK), a good looking young man nodded to him from the next table. "Who is that?" I questioned. "That is the newly married Prince Phillip." he replied. Several Royal Naval officers had joined the prince at his table and I was shocked at the way HRH had his feet up on an adjoining chair and was beating his Melton Mowbray pie with a fork to make a point in the conversation. At 17 years old, and newly married myself, I thought his behaviour was rather bad mannered. My father-in-law said gently, "Once you have learnt the rules (i.e. manners), then you can break them." Wise words indeed. Words I have had reason to use many times since then.

I'll pass on the same advice to you. Good luck and I'll see you in the Hamptons!

ABOUT THE AUTHOR

Sylvia McLaren-Tishler is the founder and director of Frameworks Training and Finishing Academy. Throughout her years training young professionals in sales and presentation skills, she found more and more of her clients requesting help in training their staff in professional protocol and etiquette. Recognizing this need, she took her certification from the Protocol School of Palm Beach and added Business protocol and Dining Decorum programs to her company resume.

She is a member of the Vancouver Board of Trade and the ESN networking groups.

A consummate networker, she is often asked by clients and friends for tips on networking, remembering names, dining etiquette and other rules of decorum. Short of having them sign up for one of her seminars, she decided to write this book of *Pocket Tips* to answer some of their questions in a hurry.

Sylvia has found that having polished manners can take you with comfort and confidence all over the world and can open doors to many opportunities that you might otherwise miss for lack of making a good impression.

She is the author of *Public Speaking for the Terrified Pocket Tips* and lives in Richmond, British Columbia, Canada with her husband, Michael, and their dog, Tess.

For more information, or to book Sylvia McLaren-Tishler for a keynote speaking engagement, visit her website at www.frameworks-training.com.

Look for Sylvia's other books:
Pocket Manners for Men
Public Speaking for the Terrified! Pocket Tips